LITTLE HOUSE

Laura Ingalls Wilder

MY FIRST LITTLE HOUSE BOOKS

MY LITTLE HOUSE COOKBOOK

ADAPTED FROM THE LITTLE HOUSE BOOKS

By Laura Ingalls Wilder

Recipes by Amy Cotler

Illustrated by Holly Jones

HARPERCOLLINS*PUBLISHERS*

For Tommy and Emma, my two true loves
—A.C.
To my mom and dad
—H. J.

Illustrations for the *My First Little House Books* are
inspired by the work of Garth Williams with his
permission, which we gratefully acknowledge.

Jacket illustration by Renée Graef
HarperCollins®, ■®, and Little House® are trademarks of HarperCollins Publishers, Inc.

Some text is adapted from the Little House books by Laura Ingalls Wilder.

Library of Congress Cataloging-in-Publication Data
Wilder, Laura Ingalls, 1867–1957.
    My Little house cookbook / adapted from the Little house books ; recipes by Amy
Cotler ; illustrated by Holly Jones.
        p.   cm. — (My First Little House books)
    Summary: A collection of favorite recipes from Laura Ingalls Wilder's Little House
books.
    ISBN 0-06-024296-5. — ISBN 0-06-024297-3 (lib. bdg.)
    1. Cookery—Juvenile literature.   2. Cookery, American—Juvenile literature.
3. Literary cookbooks—Juvenile literature. [1. Cookery, American.   2. Literary
cookbooks.] I. Cotler, Amy.   II. Jones, Holly, ill.   III. Title.   IV. Series.
TX652.5.W545   1996   94-48529
641.5'123—dc20   CIP
                                                                       AC

1   2   3   4   5   6   7   8   9   10
❖
First Edition

Once upon a time, a little girl named Laura Ingalls traveled across America in a covered wagon with her Pa, her Ma, her big sister Mary, and her little sisters Carrie and Grace. Laura and her family shared many exciting adventures as they traveled and settled in new places on the frontier. For the Ingalls family, no matter where they were, mealtime was always a cause for celebration. The family worked very hard for their food, and at each meal they would come together and give thanks for the food on their table. Here are eleven of Laura's most cherished recipes. With the help of a grown-up, you can try Laura's recipes and share your creations with your own family!

Pancakes

(about 20 small pancakes, 15 faces, or 6 full people)

Ma made a pancake man for each one of the children. It was exciting to watch her turn the whole little man over, quickly and carefully, on a hot griddle.

TOOLS

measuring cups

measuring spoons

medium-sized bowl

wooden spoon

small saucepan

small bowl

whisk

heavy frying pan

tablespoon

teaspoon

spatula

serving plate

DRY INGREDIENTS

½ cup whole wheat flour

½ cup unbleached white flour

½ teaspoon baking soda

¼ teaspoon salt

WET INGREDIENTS

2 tablespoons butter

1 egg

1 cup buttermilk

2 tablespoons maple syrup

oil or butter to cover pan

maple syrup and butter

   (or other toppings of your choice)

1. Put dry ingredients in the medium bowl. Stir until mixed.

2. Ask a grown-up to help you melt the 2 tablespoons butter in a small saucepan over medium heat.

3. Mix the melted butter, egg, buttermilk, and 2 tablespoons maple syrup together in the small bowl.

4. Add to dry ingredients. Whisk together until the mixture has almost no lumps.

5. Ask a grown-up to help you cook the pancakes. Add just enough oil or butter to the pan to cover it evenly. Pour the shapes into the pan over medium heat. Add more shapes, leaving room for the batter to expand. Once the tops bubble, slip the spatula under each pancake and look at the underside. If brown, flip over and cook the other side about half as long as the first. If needed, add more butter or oil to the pan to prevent sticking. Serve with butter and maple syrup, strawberry jam, or your own choice of toppings.

Shapes

SIMPLE STACKED PANCAKES

*Pour one full tablespoon of batter into pan
to make little pancakes that are easy to turn.
Stack the cooked pancakes onto a plate with small
pats of butter between them.*

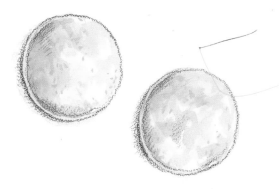

PANCAKE FACES

*Create faces using one tablespoon of batter
per face. Use drops that fall from the spoon
as eyes and nose. Spoon a crescent shape for
the mouth. When cooked, place shapes on
a plate and create your own pancake face!
For extra fun, create hair and hats.*

PANCAKE PEOPLE

*Make one person at a time. Make the body by
putting a full teaspoon of batter in the center of the pan.
Drop ½ teaspoon of batter just above the body for
the head. Add both arms from one teaspoon of batter,
then both legs from another teaspoon of batter.*

Breakfast Sausage Balls

(16 balls)

*The little pieces of meat that had been cut off the large pieces,
Ma chopped and chopped until it was all chopped fine. She seasoned it
with salt and pepper and with dried sage leaves from the garden.
With her hands she molded it into balls.*

TOOLS

measuring spoons

medium-sized bowl

peeler

grater

garlic press

10–12" frying pan

INGREDIENTS

1 pound ground pork

oregano, sage, nutmeg,
   cinnamon (2 pinches each)

1 teaspoon salt

15 grinds of black pepper

1 apple

1 garlic clove

1. Place the pork in the bowl. Sprinkle the spices, salt, and pepper on top. Ask a grown-up to help you peel the apple and grate it, using the largest holes on the grater. Next, ask a grown-up to help you peel the garlic clove and put it through the garlic press. Add the apple and garlic to the mixture.
2. Mix thoroughly with your hands. *(Do not taste until the meat is well cooked.)* Divide the mixture into 4 parts, and roll each part into 4 balls. You should have a total of 16 balls.

3. Put the sausage balls into the unheated frying pan.
4. Ask a grown-up to help you cook the balls over medium heat. Shake the pan occasionally so that they brown evenly. Cook for about 10 minutes, until centers are no longer pink and balls are cooked all the way through.

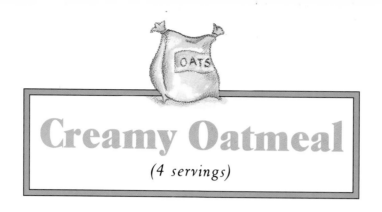

Creamy Oatmeal

(4 servings)

The big blue platter on the stove's hearth was full of plump sausage cakes;
Eliza Jane was cutting apple pies and Alice was dishing up the oatmeal, as usual.

TOOLS

measuring cups

small pot (preferably
   nonstick)

long-handled wooden spoon

4 bowls

4 spoons

INGREDIENTS

2 cups water

1 cup old-fashioned oats

pinch salt

POSSIBLE TOPPINGS

milk

maple syrup, sugar, or honey

butter

raisins

sliced bananas

crunchy wheat germ

1. Pour the water into the pot. Add the oats and salt.
2. Ask a grown-up to help you bring the mixture to a boil. Lower the heat to a simmer. Cook for 5 minutes or until the desired thickness, stirring occasionally.

3. Spoon into bowls and serve with the topping(s) of your choice.

Strawberry Jam

(about 1 cup)

Almanzo tucked his napkin deeper into the neckband of his red waist. And he ate plum preserves and strawberry jam, and grape jelly, and spiced watermelon-rind pickles.

TOOLS

measuring cup

measuring spoons

dinner knife or huller

potato masher or food
   processor

small saucepan

tablespoon

small bowl

fork or small whisk

wooden spoon

1-cup container with lid

INGREDIENTS

1 pint fresh strawberries

½ cup sugar

1 tablespoon cornstarch

½–1 teaspoon fresh
   lemon juice

1. Remove tops from strawberries and ask a grown-up to help you cut them in half, and place them in the saucepan. If berries are very ripe, mash with a potato masher until they are in small pieces. For less-ripe berries, ask a grown-up to help you place them in a food processor with a chopping blade and pulse a few times until they are in small pieces. Some can be larger than others—just make sure the mixture is not too soupy.

2. Toss the berry pieces and the sugar together in the saucepan. Let stand for 20 minutes. Press a spoon into the berry liquid and remove 1 tablespoon of the liquid. Put in the small bowl (or use the measuring cup). Using the fork or small whisk, mix the cornstarch into the tablespoon of berry liquid until there are no lumps. Add the mixture back to the berries.

3. Ask a grown-up to help you bring the berries to a boil. Stir occasionally and continue to boil mixture for about 15 minutes, or until the jam is thick (the mixture will continue to thicken a little bit, later, when you've put it in the refrigerator).

4. When the jam is cool enough to handle, spoon the mixture into the container, cover, and refrigerate. When the mixture is cold, add the lemon juice to taste and mix.

Homemade Butter

(about 3 ounces)

*Laura and Mary watched, breathless, one on each side of Ma,
while the golden little butter-pats, each with its strawberry on the top, dropped
onto the plate as Ma put all the butter through the mold.*

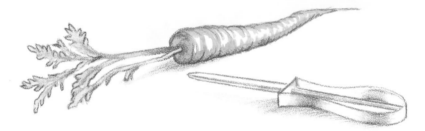

TOOLS

measuring cups

vegetable peeler

knife

food processor

small bowl

small sieve (to fit over bowl)

cheesecloth

spoon

butter mold

plastic wrap

INGREDIENTS

1 raw carrot (for color)

1 cup of heavy cream

2 cups ice water

3–5 shakes salt to taste

1. Ask a grown-up to help you peel and slice the carrot. Put the carrot, cream, and salt in the food processor and blend until cream is whipped. Add the ice water and continue to process (about 5 minutes) until the cream separates. Blend another minute.

2. Put the sieve over the bowl. Cut a tripled piece of cheesecloth that is several inches larger than the sieve, and drape it in the sieve. Empty the contents of the food processor into the cheesecloth.

3. Press and stir the mixture, getting as much liquid as possible to go through the cloth. Gather up the edges of the cloth and twist out any remaining liquid until you have a tight bundle.

4. Press the butter into a pretty butter mold, or a ⅓-cup measure lined with plastic wrap, and refrigerate. Or roll it into a log, cover with plastic wrap, chill, and cut into slices.

Butter and Jam Sandwiches

(1 sandwich)

*They all sat on the warm sand near the wagon and ate bread
and butter and cheese, hard-boiled eggs and cookies.*

TOOLS
tablespoon
butter knife
cutting board

INGREDIENTS
2 slices of bread
1 tablespoon homemade strawberry jam
1 tablespoon homemade butter
(softened to room temperature)

1. Spread jam evenly on one slice of bread, butter evenly on the other.
2. Press the jammed and buttered sides of the two slices of bread together to make a sandwich. Cut in halves or quarters.

Popcorn and Milk

(4 servings)

Almanzo looked at every kernel before he ate it. He had eaten thousands of handfuls of popcorn, and never found two kernels alike. Then he thought that if he had some milk, he would have popcorn and milk.

TOOLS

measuring cup

measuring spoons

popcorn popper or
2-quart pot
with lid

bowl for tossing

8 8-ounce glasses

4 spoons

INGREDIENTS

1 quart popped popcorn
or ¼ cup unpopped popcorn

3 tablespoons vegetable oil

½ teaspoon salt or sugar
(optional)

1 quart milk

1. If you are making it fresh, ask a grown-up to help you prepare 1 quart of popcorn. First place 1 kernel and the oil in the pot. Cover and cook over high heat until the kernel pops. Add the rest of the popcorn kernels to the pot, cover again, and cook over medium heat. Shake the pot occasionally until all the kernels are popped.

2. When the popcorn is cool enough to handle, toss with salt or sugar if you like. Completely fill four glasses with milk and four with popcorn. Give each person one popcorn glass and one milk glass. Drop the popcorn, one kernel at a time, into the milk. Slow down toward the end to give the popcorn a chance to settle.

3. When you have added all the popcorn to the milk, eat the popcorn with a spoon, and drink the milk.

Buttermilk Cornbread

(6–8 servings)

Ma made the cornmeal and water into two thin loaves, each shaped in a half circle. She laid the loaves with their straight sides together in the bake-oven, and she pressed her hand flat on top of each loaf.

TOOLS

measuring spoons

measuring cups

2 medium-sized bowls

wooden spoon

small saucepan

fork or whisk

10" greased pie plate

toothpick

DRY INGREDIENTS

1 cup flour

¾ cup stone-ground
   yellow cornmeal

1 teaspoon baking soda

1 teaspoon baking powder

½ teaspoon salt

¼ cup brown sugar

WET INGREDIENTS

3 tablespoons butter

2 eggs

1½ cups buttermilk

butter to serve on bread

1. Ask a grown-up to help you preheat the oven to 425°.
2. Combine all dry ingredients in one bowl. Mix well with the wooden spoon, breaking up any sugar lumps with your fingers.
3. Ask a grown-up to help you melt the 3 tablespoons butter in a small saucepan over medium heat.

4. Combine wet ingredients in the second bowl: First, break the eggs in the bottom of the bowl. Next, add the buttermilk and then the melted butter to the bowl. With the tines of the fork or small whisk, break the yolks, then beat the liquid until well combined.
5. Mix the wet into the dry ingredients until just blended. Pour into the pie plate.

6. Bake for 20 minutes, or until an inserted toothpick comes out clean. Cut into wedges and serve warm with plenty of butter.

Laura's Little Maple Cakes

(24 mini-cupcakes)

*The cakes were too pretty to eat. Mary and Laura just
looked at them. But at last Laura turned hers over, and she nibbled
a tiny nibble from underneath, where it wouldn't show.*

TOOLS

measuring cups

measuring spoons

small saucepan

3 medium-sized bowls

whisk

2 12-mini-muffin nonstick pans

wooden spoon or hand-held mixer

plates or little cups for toppings

DRY INGREDIENTS

1¼ cups flour

½ teaspoon baking soda

pinch salt

½ teaspoon ginger

WET INGREDIENTS

2 tablespoons unsalted butter

½ cup maple syrup

1 egg

½ cup sour cream

butter (to grease the tins)

1. Ask a grown-up to help you preheat the oven to 375°, and to help you melt the 2 tablespoons butter in the small saucepan over medium heat.

2. Put dry ingredients into one bowl and mix. Combine wet ingredients in another bowl and whisk together. Add the wet to the dry ingredients. Mix quickly, just until thoroughly blended.

3. Grease the muffin tins and fill them, using two tablespoons, one to scoop the batter, the other to push it off into the tin.

4. Bake for 12 minutes, or until the cakes are a light golden color. When they are cool enough to handle, remove from the pans.

Maple Icing

    1 cup confectioner's sugar
    ½ tablespoon unsalted butter, softened
    pinch salt
    ¼ teaspoon vanilla
    ⅓ cup maple syrup

5. To make maple icing, blend sugar, butter, salt, and vanilla. Add maple syrup and beat until completely smooth.

6. Decorate each cake by dipping the top of each into the icing and giving it a twist. Turn it right side up, and while the icing is still moist, garnish with a variety of toppings.

Toppings

(choose at least three kinds for each cake)

- 2 shakes multicolored sprinkles
- slice of strawberry
- whole raspberry or blueberry
- ½ seedless grape (dipped in sugar)
- 1 dried currant
- ⅛ teaspoon strawberry jam
- edible flowers (unsprayed): violet, red
or white clover, pansy, lilac, or lavender
Use your imagination!

Ma's Best
Butter Cookies

(about 25 cookies)

*Ma baked vinegar pies and dried-apple pies, and filled
a big jar with cookies, and she let Laura and Mary lick the cake spoon.*

TOOLS

measuring cups

measuring spoons

small bowl

large bowl

tablespoon or wooden spoon

baking sheet

fork

spatula

wire rack

airtight tin

INGREDIENTS

1½ cups flour

½ teaspoon salt

½ teaspoon baking soda

½ teaspoon powdered ginger

1 stick unsalted butter,
    room temperature

½ cup light brown sugar

1 egg

1 teaspoon vanilla

2 tablespoons sugar or
    multicolored sprinkles

1. Ask a grown-up to help you preheat the oven to 375°.

2. Put the flour, salt, baking soda, and ginger into the small bowl and mix lightly.

3. Use a sturdy tablespoon or a large wooden spoon to cream the butter and sugar: First mash the softened butter thoroughly in the large bowl. Next, add the brown sugar and mash the butter and sugar together until they are soft and completely combined.

4. Add the egg and vanilla to the butter and sugar and mix together well. Empty the bowl of dry ingredients into the wet mixture. Keep stirring until thoroughly combined. Finish off with your hands if you'd like, mixing until the dough is one uniform light-brown color.

5. Put the 2 tablespoons of sugar or sprinkles into the bowl that held the flour mixture. Wash your hands and don't dry them. Roll walnut-sized balls of dough.

6. Press one side into the sugar or sprinkles, coating the top generously. Place the balls, topping side up, 1½" apart, on the cookie sheet. Press the fork into the top of each cookie.

7. Bake for 12 minutes or until cookies are lightly browned. Remove with the spatula and place on a rack to cool. Store in the airtight tin.

Lemonade

(4 servings)

"Is your lemonade sweet enough?" Mrs. Oleson asked. So Laura knew that it was lemonade in the glasses. She had never tasted anything like it.

TOOLS

measuring cups

pitcher

long-handled spoon

fork, lemon reamer, or juicer

knife

4 glasses

INGREDIENTS

½ cup sugar

1 cup hot tap water

2 lemons

2 cups cold water

10 ice cubes

4 lemon slices

1. Pour the sugar into the pitcher. Ask a grown-up to help you add the hot tap water to the sugar. Stir about 20 times to dissolve the sugar. Ask a grown-up to help you cut the lemons in half and, using the lemon reamer or juicer, extract ½ cup of lemon juice. Add the lemon juice, the cold water, and the ice cubes to the mixture. Stir to combine.

2. To garnish, drop a lemon slice into each glass, or make a slit to the center of each slice and stand it up on the rim of each glass.

Index

of Recipes